Who Grows Up in the Forest?

A Book About Forest Animals and Their Offspring

Written by Theresa Longenecker
Illustrated by Melissa Carpenter

Content Advisor: Julie Dunlap, Ph.D.
Reading Advisor: Lauren A. Liang, M.A.
Literacy Education, University of Minnesota
Minneapolis, Minnesota

PICTURE WINDOW BOOKS
Minneapolis, Minnesota

Designer: Melissa Voda
Page production: The Design Lab
The illustrations in this book were prepared digitally.

Picture Window Books
5115 Excelsior Boulevard
Suite 232
Minneapolis, MN 55416
1-877-845-8392
www.picturewindowbooks.com

Printed in the United States of America.

Library of Congress Cataloging-in-Publication Data
Longenecker, Theresa, 1955–
  Who grows up in the forest? : a book about forest animals and their offspring / written by Theresa
Longenecker ; illustrated by Melissa Carpenter.
    p. cm.
  Summary: Names and describes the offspring of a squirrel, toad, woodpecker, wolf, opossom, bear,
mouse, and whitetail deer.
  ISBN 1-4048-0025-5 (lib. bdg. : alk. paper)
  1. Forest animals—Infancy—Juvenile literature. [1. Forest animals—Infancy.] I. Carpenter, Melissa, ill.
II. Title.
  QL112 .L66 2003
  599.139—dc21
                                                                                2002006285

Many baby animals grow up in the forest. Some live in burrows or dens in the ground. Others nest high in the trees. Babies might be born in a cave, a pond, or a shady nest. Some baby animals stay near their parents. Others go off on their own.

Let's read about some baby animals that grow up in the forest.

Kitten

A baby gray squirrel is called a kitten.

Squirrel kittens are born with their eyes and ears closed. They cuddle up to their mother's soft, furry body to stay warm and drink her milk. They can see and hear when they are about one month old.

5

6

Tadpole

A baby American toad is called a tadpole.

Tadpoles hatch from eggs that the mother toad laid in a pond. Tadpoles look like little fish. They have big heads and long tails. Within two months, the tadpoles grow legs and start to look like adult toads.

Did you know?
A mother toad lays up to 20,000 eggs at a time. She lays them as she swims through the water, leaving behind a long string of tiny black eggs.

Nestling

A baby pileated woodpecker is called a nestling.

These three woodpecker nestlings will stay in the nest for almost one month. They get food from their parents. The nestlings open their beaks, and the mother or father woodpecker coughs up insects for them to swallow.

Pup

A baby gray wolf is called a pup.

Newborn pups stay with their mother in the den. They drink her milk, and she cares for them. After a few weeks, the pups are old enough to leave the den and meet the rest of the family, or pack.

Did you know?
The whole pack pitches in to hunt
for food for the pups and protect
them from enemies.

Joey

A baby Virginia opossum is called a joey.

Right after birth, opossum joeys crawl into a pouch on their mother's belly. They stay there for two months, nursing and growing. Then they crawl in and out of the pouch. Soon they can ride on their mother's back.

Did you know?
A young opossum can wrap its tail tightly around a branch and hang upside down. Older opossums are too heavy to hang this way.

Cub

A baby American black bear is called a cub.

Black bear cubs are born while their mother is in her winter sleep. For the rest of the winter, they stay in the den — sleeping, nursing, and growing. When spring comes, they follow their mother outside. Sometimes they ride on her back.

Fawn

A baby whitetail deer is called a fawn.

Fawns have white spots on their coats. The spots help them blend in with the splashes of sunlight on the forest floor. Most fawns are born in the spring. By autumn, their coats lose their spots.

Did you know?

Male fawns, called bucks, have little bumps on their heads. These bumps grow into antlers.

Pinkie

A baby white-footed mouse is called a pinkie.

These pinkies latch on to their mother to drink her milk. If the mother gets scared while they are feeding, the pinkies just hold on as she runs. At birth, they are helpless and blind, but only one week later they can see and move about.

Fast Facts

Gray Squirrel: If the mother squirrel needs to move a kitten, she gently picks it up in her mouth. She grabs the kitten by the tummy, and the kitten curls around her neck. When they are three months old, squirrel kittens leave the nest and hunt for food on their own. Their favorite foods are nuts, insects, fruits, seeds, flowers, and mushrooms.

American Toad: Even though tadpoles look like fish, they aren't strong enough to swim until they are a few days old. Once they are grown, they live mostly on land. American toads are short and fat. Their skin is thick, dry, and bumpy. They rest in cool, dark places, sometimes under leaves or stones. American toads also dig burrows in the ground to escape the summer heat or winter cold. A toad often sits at the opening to its burrow and slurps up passing insects with its tongue.

Pileated Woodpecker: Woodpecker parents make a nest by pecking out a hole in a tree. After the nestlings hatch, the mother watches them during the day. The father watches them at night. Woodpeckers have sharp hearing. They can hear insects moving and chewing deep inside a tree. The birds peck holes to get to the insects. Then they use their sticky tongues with little bristles at the end to pick up the insects. Woodpeckers also eat berries, seeds, nuts, eggs, and even mice.

Gray Wolf: There are usually about six pups in a gray wolf's litter. The pups are born in the spring and are reared in a den. The other wolves in the pack leave food for the mother while she is nursing the helpless pups. By October, a pup is ready to hunt and travel with the pack. A wolf pack can have as many as 15 members. One main pair—a male and a female—leads the pack. These wolves are usually the strongest and the best hunters.

Virginia Opossum: About 5 to 17 tiny Virginia opossum joeys are born at one time. The opossum is the only land animal in North America to carry its young in a pouch like a kangaroo. When joeys are about four months old, they leave the pouch for good and learn to hunt. Opossums hunt at night and sleep during the day. They eat fruit, earthworms, frogs, lizards, mice, dead animals, or insects.

American Black Bear: Two or three cubs are born at a time in a den. Their den can be a hollow tree, a cave, or a hole in the ground. Newborns are blind, deaf, and almost hairless. After three months, the cubs can follow their mother out of the den. If there is danger, they run back into their den or scramble up a tree. "Black bear" is the name for a kind of bear, but black bears are not always black. They can be brown, reddish brown, silver gray, or even tan. Black bears eat almost anything, but they especially like berries, nuts, and insects.

Whitetail Deer: Whitetail does (DOHS), or female deer, often have twins. Newborn fawns drink their mother's milk. After two or three weeks, they begin munching on green plants. A deer's sense of smell is so keen that the deer usually smells an enemy before it sees any sign of the danger. A whitetail deer can run very fast and jump over high fences. The white underside of its tail flashes like a flag behind it.

White-footed Mouse: Pinkies grow up quickly. They stop nursing after three or four weeks. When females are only eight weeks old, they are ready to have their own babies. White-footed mice might make their homes in forgotten bird nests, or they might find burrows in the ground. Like cats, these mice often lick their faces, paws, and whiskers. They also stalk and pounce on insects. White-footed mice carry seeds in their cheeks and hide stores of food for later. They are most active at night.

Forest Babies at a Glance

Word for Baby	Animal	Born How	First Food	Word for Female	Word for Male	Word for Group
Kitten	Gray squirrel	Live	Mother's milk	Doe	Buck	Drey
Tadpole	American toad	Egg	Algae, plants	Female	Male	Knot
Nestling	Pileated woodpecker	Egg	Insects	Female	Male	——
Pup	Gray wolf	Live	Mother's milk	Female	Dog	Pack
Joey	Virgina opossum	Live	Mother's milk	Female	Male	——
Cub	Black bear	Live	Mother's milk	Sow	Boar	Family
Fawn	Whitetail deer	Live	Mother's milk	Doe	Buck	Herd
Pinkie	White-footed mouse	Live	Mother's milk	Female	Male	Horde

Where Do They Live?

Gray squirrel — North American forests and urban areas

American toad — North American woodlands, yards, and fields

Pileated woodpecker — central Canada to as far south as Florida and Texas

Gray wolf — Canada, northern Wisconsin and Minnesota, Yellowstone Park, and Alaska

Virginia opossum — eastern United States to Colorado, as far north as Minnesota and Wisconsin

American black bear — Canada, United States, and Mexico

Whitetail deer — central Canada to northern South America

White-footed mouse — brushy woodlands of eastern North America, southern Canada, and Mexico

Make an Ice Wreath for the Birds and Squirrels

What You Need

Pan with a center tube
(such as an angel
food cake pan)

Shortening

Water

Twigs and sticks

Cranberries

Seeds

Nuts

A freezer

What to Do

1. Rub a thin coat of shortening on the inside of the pan. This will keep your ice wreath from sticking to the pan.

2. Fill the pan with 2 inches (5 centimeters) of water.

3. Place twigs and sticks in the water.

4. Sprinkle berries, seeds, and nuts in the water.

5. Place the pan in the freezer and freeze overnight.

6. Take the pan out of the freezer. Remove the ice wreath by setting the pan in warm water, just until the edges of the wreath melt and loosen.

7. Hang the ice wreath from a sturdy branch or fence post. Birds and squirrels will pick at the ice wreath and eat the berries, seeds, and nuts.

Words to Know

antler—one of two branching, bony forms on the head of some animals such as male deer

beak—a bird's mouth. A woodpecker uses its beak to peck trees for insects.

burrow—a hole or tunnel in the ground made by an animal, usually for its home

den—the home of some wild animals, such as bears

nurse—to drink mother's milk

pack—a group of wolves or other animals that live and hunt together

pouch—a pocket on the front of some animals' bodies where their babies nurse and begin to grow. An opossum has a pouch.

To Learn More

Index

At the Library

Bair, Diane, and Pamela Wright. *Deer Watching.* Mankato, Minn.: Capstone Press, 2000.

Klingel, Cynthia Fitterer, and Robert B. Noyed. *Forests.* Chanhassen, Minn.: Child's World, 2002.

Schaefer, Lola M. *Wolves: Life in the Pack.* Mankato, Minn.: Bridgestone Books, 2001.

On the Web

FactHound offers a safe, fun way to find Web sites related to this book. All of the sites on FactHound have been researched by our staff.
www.facthound.com

1. Visit the FactHound home page.

2. Enter a search word related to this book, or type in this special code: 1404800255.

3. Click the FETCH IT button.

Your trusty FactHound will fetch the best Web sites for you!